Who Is Maxine Waters

Waters was born in 1938 in Kinloch, Missouri, the daughter of Velma Lee and Remus Carr. Fifth out of thirteen children, Waters was raised by her single mother once her father left the family when Maxine was two.

She graduated from Vashon High School in St. Louis, Missouri before moving with her family to Los Angeles, California in 1961. She worked in a garment factory and as a telephone operator before being hired as an assistant teacher with the Head Start program at Watts in 1966. Waters later enrolled at Los Angeles State College, where she received a sociology undergraduate degree in 1970.

Maxine Moore Waters currently serves as the U.S. Representative for California's 43rd congressional district, and previously served the 35th and 29th districts, serving in Congress since 1991.

A member of the Democratic Party, she is the most senior of the 12 black women currently serving in the United States Congress, and is a member and former chair of the Congressional Black Caucus. Before becoming a member of Congress, she served in the California Assembly, to which she was first elected in 1976. As an Assembly member.

Ms. Waters represents the 43rd district of Los Angeles, formerly known as South Central. While gang violence may not be as prevalent as it was two decades ago, that doesn't mean areas around South Central, L.A. are completely safe. Crime such as armed robbery is more likely to occur in South Central than other areas of the city.

Several travel guides suggest, it is best to avoid Compton, Gardena, and other portions of South Central at night. Armed robbery and breaking into vehicles is more likely to happen at night.

In South Los Angeles you have a 1 in 23 chance of becoming a victim of crime. South Central has a higher crime rate than the national average in all types of crime. Violent crime is especially concerning as the violent crime rate is nearly triple the national average.

South Central was the home to turf wars between rival gangs in the 1970's-1990's. The Zoot Suit Riot, Watts Riot, and Rodney King Riot all took place in South Central.

Los Angeles is one of only two major U.S. metropolitan areas in which concentrated poverty became more prevalent between 1990 and 2000.

The City Council voted unanimously to take South Central Los Angeles off the map, renaming the historically black area in an effort to divorce it from an international image of riots, poverty, and gang crime.

Rather than fix the crime stricken area, the council changed the name to South Los Angeles, which will appear in all future city documents and on city maps.

Despite almost 40 years of Ms. Waters leadership, or perhaps because of it, little positive change has occurred in her district.

A member of the U.S. House of Representatives is constitutionally required to only live in the state which they represent. However, there is a strongly followed unwritten convention that House members maintain a residence in the district they represent, and it is highly uncommon for a member not to do so.

Ms. Waters is one of those highly uncommon members. While she proclaims to advocate for the rights of the poor, and often infers that she herself is part of their struggle, she does not live amongst her constituents. She lives in a mansion in one of the most affluent areas of Los Angeles, Hancock Park. Her neighbors include, Antonio Banderas, Natalie Cole, Lou Rawls, Mindy Kaling, and Melanie Griffith.

The Average price for a 4-bedroom house in Hancock Park is 3 million dollars. Maxine Waters home is estimated to be valued at 4.5 million dollars.

Waters also owns two other homes valued at over a million dollars each. Ms. Waters becomes very defensive when people question how she can afford such an affluent lifestyle on a government salary. She has never given a rational explanation preferring to accuse the questioner of racism.

With each passing day, the American people learn more about the rampant corruption in the Democratic party. For so long we have heard the left say that they are morally superior to Republicans. However, while that sounds insane there are so many people out there that buy it.

At any rate, these corrupt politicians act like they care about the average American, but their actions say otherwise. Their only concern has been about power and money which is pathetic. Though there is one individual on the left that truly encompasses the corruption of the Democratic party besides Hillary Clinton, and that award goes to Democratic Rep. Maxine Waters.

Corruption: The art of getting away with things while pointing your fingers at others

Citizens for Responsibility and Ethics in Washington (CREW) is a nonprofit organization dedicated to promoting ethics and accountability in government and public life by targeting government officials, regardless of party affiliation who sacrifice the common good to special interests. It's important to note that CREW is a liberal organization, but it does fairly expose people on both sides of the aisle. CREW creates an annual list of the most corrupt members of congress. Maxine waters has made the list many times.

According to Phillip, Joshua, 2017, *An eight-page CREW report lists her numerous cases of misconduct, and the investigations into her actions. Among the cases, she allegedly "used her position as a senior member of Congress and member of the House Financial Services Committee to prevail upon Treasury officials to meet with One United Bank," says CREW.*

Judicial Watch, Inc., a conservative, non-partisan educational foundation, promotes transparency, accountability and integrity in government, politics, and the law. Judicial Watch advocates high standards of ethics and morality in our nation's public life and seeks to ensure that political and judicial officials do not abuse the powers entrusted to them by the American people.

It's important to note that Judicial Watch is a conservative organization, but it does fairly expose people on both sides of the aisle. As with CREW, Judicial Watch also creates an annual list of the most corrupt members of congress. Maxine waters has made the list many times.

According to Phillip, Joshua, 2017, Judicial Watch, referred to Waters in Dec. 10, 2012, as "A famously corrupt, and seemingly untouchable, congresswoman renowned for abusing her power to enrich family members," and criticized her rise to become a ranking member of the House Financial Services Committee.

Given that her corruption is well known in Washington and much of the country, it is curious how she continues to have the support of voters in her district.

According to Phillip, Joshua, 2017, An eight-page CREW report lists her numerous cases of misconduct, and the investigations into her actions.

Among the cases, Waters allegedly used her position as a senior member of Congress and member of the House Financial Services Committee to prevail upon Treasury officials to meet with One United Bank.

The House Ethics Committee investigated Waters for steering $12 million in federal bailout funds to a failing Massachusetts bank that she and her husband a board member held shares in.

The New York Times noted her unexpected rise to fame on the left stating "Through all the tumult, Ms. Waters, once deemed 'one of the most corrupt members of Congress' by a liberal watchdog group, has remade herself from Los Angeles ward politician to a darling of the left."

According to Schmidt, Susan, 2009, *Ms. Waters and her husband have both held financial stakes in the bank. Until recently, her husband was a director. At the same time, Ms. Waters has publicly boosted One United's executives and criticized its government regulators during congressional hearings. Last fall, she helped secure the bank a meeting with Treasury officials.*

Such potential conflicts of interest are more serious as the banking system's crisis has led the government to take an increasingly active role in overseeing financial institutions, including One United. The financial-services committee, on which Ms. Waters sits, oversees banking issues, and the lawmaker is a potential future chairman.

Ms. Waters should have recused herself from any matters involving the bank. If her support helped One United. Ms. Waters and her husband, Sidney Williams, were investors in two African-American owned California banks that merged with other lenders in 2002 to form One United. Congressional financial-disclosure forms show Ms. Waters acquired One United stock worth between $250,000 and $500,000 in March 2004, as did Mr. Williams. Mr. Williams joined the board of One United that year.

In a brief interview in January, Ms. Waters said she was unaware the bank received $12 million of TARP money, which arrived in December. One United was "just a small" bank, she said.

A provision designed to aid One United was written into the federal bailout legislation by

Barney Frank, who is chairman of the financial-services panel.

According to Coca, Anan, 2017, In 2010, Waters was brought up on three separate charges by her colleagues in the House, even after Rep. Barney Frank warned Waters against getting involved in advocating for a bank in which she had financial interest.

The investigative panel said Waters, who sits on the Financial Services Committee, broke a House rule requiring members to behave in a way that reflects "creditably" in the chamber. The committee said that by trying to assist One United, Waters stood to benefit directly, because her husband owned a sizable amount of stock that would have been "worthless" if the bank failed.

The committee also accused Waters of violating the "spirit" of a House rule prohibiting lawmakers from using their positions for financial gain, as well as a government ethics statute banning the dispensing of "special favors."

According to America Rising PAC, 2016, Congresswoman Maxine Waters has long had a troubled relationship with the rules. During the financial crisis, Waters used her high-

Amid a national financial catastrophe, Rep. Maxine Waters used her position as a senior member of Congress and member of the House Financial Services Committee to prevail upon Treasury officials to meet with One United Bank. She never disclosed that her husband held stock in the bank.

*The House Ethics Committee investigated
Waters and her office, and eventually
reprimanded her chief of staff, who happens
to be her grandson.*

According to the P.A., ENV News, 2017,
*Waters has spread out her nefarious deeds to
include her daughter, Karen Waters. Rep.
Waters is slated to pay her daughter another
$108,000 for running a lucrative campaign
operation that pulls in hundreds of thousands
of dollars each election cycle. This behavior
was unnecessary because Waters has access
to a national campaign fund that does not
cost the taxpayers anything.*

*That was not good enough for greedy Waters.
She hired her daughter to run what is called a
slate mailer scheme that essentially forces
candidates running for office to pay Waters
for access to her far-reaching publicity
campaign. When Waters pays her daughter a
six-figure balance owed her, she will have
given Karen Waters around $750,000 for
running the mailers for the campaign since
2006.*

*Instead of using money from the national
campaign fund, Maxine decided to use
taxpayer's money to pay her daughter for the
campaign.*

*This is a level of obvious graft that should
outrage all Americans because of its abuse of
power, hypocrisy, and the self-righteous*

sense of entitlement displayed by the Waters girls.

Karen pulled in $65,287 overseeing the slate mailer operation in 2016, making her the third-largest recipient of Waters campaign funds that cycle. But things get more corrupt.

According to Phillips, Joshua, 2017, *Waters has come under fire for skirting federal elections rules with a shady fundraising gimmick that allows her to receive unlimited amounts of donations from certain contributors, and for making hundreds of thousands of dollars in short periods of time by selling her endorsement to other politicians and political causes.*

According to L.B. Conservative Politicus, 2017, *Senator Kamala Harris funneled about $90,000 into Waters' campaign budget from 2010 to 2016. Harris was looking for a campaign endorsement in Waters' mailing list, and naturally, Waters was not about to just support her for free.*

There are a lot of things wrong with this narrative, there were two points where money was swapped, first in 2010, weighing $63,000, and later on, in 2016, for the sum of

$30,000. That is a large amount of money just to appear on a mailing list.

We cannot help but ask where did that money come from, and the reason behind why it was so readily sent into Waters' already thick wallet. One would have to guess that Senator Harris paid for her endorsement with tax money.

In addition, we must question if all those on her mailing list paid Waters to appear there. If they did, how much did they pay? More, less, or about the exact sum as Harris? We know that from the beginning of the pay for play mailer procedure, Waters got around $750,000 from it. Not bad for a small side project managed by Waters' daughter.

The slate mailer operation "legally" allowed Waters to bypass the campaign contribution limits. So, Harris can pay her this insane amount money to appear on her mailer since it is not considered a contribution. Leave it to the corrupt Congresswoman to find the loophole that allows her to line her own pockets.

Waters also used her influence to have her husband assigned Ambassador to the Bahamas. His qualifications were… he visited there once.

Crazy:
Mad Maxine
In her own words.

Much of what Maxine Waters says is nonsensical. It may be a jumble of incomplete thoughts, ramblings, or emotional vitriol. Her speeches are confusing but are usually random, entertaining, and unpredictable.

Occasionally, the listener can decipher one of Maxine Waters' confusing messages. Unfortunately, her messages are often so disconnected from mainstream views that confusion would have been preferable.

The following pages are filled with quotes from Maxine Waters and an interpretation of what she may have been trying to say as well as an analysis of where she missed the mark.

When Maxine Waters was asked why she was participating in the Women's March, she may not have fully thought out her response.

"I have to march because my mother could not have an abortion." (Maxine Waters)

She likely meant to say that women today have greater rights than they once did, and it is important to remember the progress women have made. Instead she took the entire rights movement and linked it to abortion. Not all women are pro-abortion. It doesn't make them any less women.

Women's rights include the right to work, vote, hold public office, attend college, earn scholarships, and be respected as equal citizens.

There is a bigger problem with this quote though. There is a disconnect to what abortion means. If her mother had an abortion, Maxine would not be here to march.

The question then becomes, does Maxine really hate herself that much, or is it her siblings she hates?

"Guess what this liberal would be all about? This liberal will be about socializing...uh, um...Would be about, basically, taking over, and the government running all of your companies." **(Maxine Waters)**

Ms. Waters has the let proverbial cat out of the socialist bag. In a genuine moment, she revealed both the contempt she and others like her have for private enterprise, and the arrogance of politicians who believe more government is the solution for everything.

The central lie of liberalism is the belief that self-interest and selfishness are the same. The people in Congress, many of whom have never done an honest day's work for an honest day's pay in their entire lives, under-estimate the importance of those who keep the country working.

If you nationalize the oil industry and the people in it decide they don't want to work for the government oil company, production stops.

There was a time in this country when the statement made by Ms. Waters would have been met with disgust and astonishment. Tragically, far too many Americans no longer recoil at the notion of socialism. They have an entitlement mind-set.

"If sequestration takes place, that's going to be a great setback. We don't need to be having something like sequestration that's going to cause these job losses — over 170 million jobs that could be lost." **(Maxine Waters)**

The term sequestration is used to define mandatory spending cuts in the federal budget. Sequestration is a mechanism used when the cost of running the government exceeds either an arbitrary amount or the gross revenue it brings during the fiscal year. There have been numerous examples of sequestration in American history.

Simply put, sequestration involves across-the-board spending cuts to reduce annual budget deficits.

Ms. Water's must think that our country is communist or socialist and that the government controls every industry. She also must think that there are 170 million jobs in the United States. There are approximately 136 million jobs in this country.

It is very unlikely that forcing congress to stay within a budget would cause every U.S. citizen (and I guess Canadians as well b her count) to lose their jobs. It just fixes our budget.

"Policy, for the most part, has been made by white people in America, not by people of color. And they have tended to take care of those things that they think are important. Whether it's their agricultural subsidies, or other kinds of expenditures that are certainly not expenditures for poor people or for people of color. And so, we have to band together and keep fighting back." **(Maxine Waters)**

Ms. Waters is correct to a point when she discusses congressional demographics. Congress, even at its most diverse has had 20% minority members. It is, however, not an exclusive club. Those voted in by citizens, are welcomed in, regardless of gender or race.

Aside from that point, she loses focus. She complains because congress members tend to take care of things they think are important. Congress members are elected to take care of things they think are important.

She then made specific mention of agriculture subsidies. Both rich and poor people depend upon a stable food supply to survive. The United States subsidizes farmers because most people realize that prices need to remain stable as does production. A bad crop year can cause farmers to not be able to produce the next year.

The United States produces an abundance of food for domestic and world consumption. Failure of production impacts the entire world. Looking towards countries that do not have subsidies for farmers shows us that there is an inconsistent production of food, and prices fluctuate greatly, often resulting in famine.

Not all farmers get subsidies, but some do. Those that do, receive 40,000 a year per farmer and a maximum of 80,000 per couple. Many of Ms. Waters constituents receive subsidized government assistance for things such as housing, food, health care, college tuition, worker training, phones, electricity; all while providing no common benefit to our country. The cost of welfare is tantamount to the subsidy to farmers.

Waters claims we all must band together and keep fighting back but doesn't specify what she wants people to back against, cheap, stable food supply or the subsidies her constituents already receive.

"Why do you think [Russians] hacked into our election? Because they have to make sure that Donald Trump got elected so that he could help them with what I think is a huuuuge deal, not only to lift these sanctions, but to take over, y'know, all of these Soviet countries and pull 'em back into the Soviet Union, so that they could have access it to all of these resources. It's clear to me!" **(Maxine Waters)**

Beginning with the obvious, there are no Soviet countries, zero, none. If there were, it would make little sense for President Trump to want to pull 'em back into the Soviet Union.

There never was any evidence to suggest the Russians hacked into our election. It is simply a rallying call by the left to justify why Clinton lost the election. Repetition may make it seem like the truth to feeble minded people, such as Ms. Waters.

There is no evidence of any collusion between President Trump and the Russians as alleged by the left. We do, however know large amounts of money went to Clinton and Obama prior to the transfer of control of Uranium deposits to the Russians. If the Russians were to influence the election it would be in favor of someone, like Clinton, who they knew was open to bribes.

Furthermore, the one way the Russians did influence the election was by purchasing advertising on social media. Those ads tended to be more beneficial to Clinton not Donald Trump.

As far as the sanctions go, the sanctions have crippled our relationship with Russia. The point of sanctions is to force another country to do something, but these sanctions were random. There was no stipulation on what Russia was required to do to have the sanctions removed. The sanctions are in nobody's best interest and should be removed.

"The anger that you see expressed out there in Los Angeles, in my district this evening, is a righteous anger, and it's difficult for me to say to the people, "Don't be angry." When people are angry and enraged, they do senseless things. They do act even sometimes out of character, and that's why it is the responsibility of America to try and avoid putting people in these kinds of situations." (**Maxine Waters**)

"Righteous anger" is an interesting term. It is unlikely that anyone aside from Waters has tried to pair these two words together. Righteous means virtuous, ethical, upstanding, and decent. Anger means a strong feeling of annoyance, displeasure, or hostility.

There was nothing righteous about the Rodney King riots. Waters says that when people are angry, the do senseless things. By the time the ashes had settled, 53 people were dead, over 4000 people were injured and over a billion dollars' worth of damage had been done.

The community impact was long lasting. Businesses, many black-owned were destroyed, along with the dream of those who had saved to become business owners and serve the community. Those living in the community no longer had convenient places to shop. Businesses that could rebuild often chose to rebuild elsewhere. People in the community who were employed by those businesses lost their jobs.

Those who could not rebuild, returned to government assistance. No righteousness here.

People who were not black became instant targets for violence. Many were caught unaware and had not known anything about the verdict or ensuing riot.

On April 29, 1992, Reginald Denny loaded his red dump truck with 27 tons of sand and began driving to a plant in Inglewood, where the sand was due. He left the Santa Monica Freeway and took a familiar shortcut across Florence Avenue to get to his destination. His truck had no radio, so he did not realize that he was driving into a riot. Rioters threw rocks at his windows, people were shouting at him to stop, forcing him to do so. Antoine Miller climbed up and opened the truck door, giving an unidentified man the chance to pull

Denny out and throw him on the ground. Henry
Watson stood on Denny's neck to hold him down
as a group of men surrounded him and Anthony
Brown kicked him in the abdomen. Miller
searched Denny's back pockets before climbing
into the truck and running off with a stolen bag. As
Watson walked away, two other unidentified men
joined in the attack: one hurled a five-pound
oxygenator stolen from another truck at Denny's
head, and the other kicked him and hit him with a
claw hammer. As Denny tried to stand up, Damian
Williams threw a piece of brick at the side of his
head, which knocked him unconscious. Williams
pointed and laughed at Denny, did a victory dance
in the road, and flashed gang signs at news
helicopters, who were televising the events live
from a helicopter.

Brown joined Williams in flashing gang signs and spat on Denny. One man stood over him, filming Denny as he lay bleeding on the ground but did not try to help him. Denny remained on the ground next to his truck, bloodied and unconscious as some residents threw bottles at him. Gary Williams approached Denny and rifled through his pockets before fleeing. As Denny slowly came to and got to his knees, the man who had earlier assaulted him with a hammer ran up and gave him a flying kick to the face. On the other side of the truck, Lance Parker stopped on his motorcycle and attempted to shoot the fuel tank with a shotgun but missed.

Bobby Green Jr., Lei Yuille, and Titus Murphy and Terri Barnett came to Denny's aid. Denny eventually dragged himself back into the cab, and drove away from the scene slowly and erratically. Green boarded Denny's truck and drove him to the Hospital.

Paramedics who attended to Denny said he came very close to death. Soon after Green brought Denny to the hospital, he suffered a seizure. His skull was fractured in 91 places and pushed into his brain. His left eye was so badly dislocated that it would have fallen into his sinus cavity had the surgeons not replaced the crushed bone with a piece of plastic. A permanent crater remains in his forehead despite efforts to correct it. There was nothing righteous here.

The "righteous anger", even lashed out at those who were there to help. Firefighters were attacked and kept from keeping citizens safe. They were shot at, attacked with axes, blocked from reaching fires and had objects thrown at them.

According to North, J., 2012, *Firefighters say they had never experienced anything like the Los Angeles riots, and they haven't since. They were shot at, had things thrown at them and had to be escorted by heavily armed police and the highway patrol.*

The mobs kept the Los Angeles Fire Department from doing what they were trained to do.

"On that day, we were like the enemy, where they didn't want us to put the fires out," said LAFD Capt. Paul Seborn.

As a result, they couldn't really fight the fires. They had to stay back away from the buildings. LAFD Capt. Scott Miller was shot in the cheek and lost the dexterity in one hand.

"The bullet traveled along my jaw and went into my neck, severed the carotid artery and lodged midline in my throat. At that point, I suffered a stroke and went face first onto the steering wheel," Miller said.

Seborn and his crew found their first stop at the intersection of Manchester and Vermont avenues in flames, and they had to let it burn.

"There was a mob of about 100 people coming toward us, and as we pulled down the street to try and set up for the fire attack, we took some shots, and we got a gunshot into the side of my door," Seborn said.

It was the first time in the firefighters' careers that they'd been made targets, and they were forced to wear ballistic vests. They couldn't do what they'd signed up for - fighting the fires and protecting the neighborhoods.

Only a few firefighters at the time got bulletproof vests. Now, they are issued to everyone in the department. The riots were a dangerous and scary time for them.

"The battalion chief was in front of me, and I saw a flash off to the right ... I saw his window blow out, and he fell over. It was a shotgun that had taken out his window," said LAFD Battalion Chief Dennis Waters. "Luckily it was a shotgun and not a rifle or a pistol."

The chief took pellets in his face. But it was not only dangerous for them, it was dangerous for the people they were trying to protect.

Eventually, they had armed guards and could spend more time trying to put out the fires that threatened people and neighborhoods. But as one firefighter says, that wasn't the way they liked to do it.

Ms. Waters could have been a calming presence but instead justified the actions of people who were destroying every vestige of the district she represents.

The media is also to blame for selectively editing a powerful video showing a black motorist being beaten. The full video showed a different picture than what has become ingrained in most people's minds. The edited video does not show the 115 miles car chase, it does not show the officers trying to peacefully de-escalate a man who showed signs of being on strong drugs. It does not show the suspect being tasered without effect.

The full, unedited video does.

According to Gray, Madison 2007, *While driving down the 210 freeway in Los Angeles with two friends, Rodney King was detected speeding by the California Highway Patrol. Fearing that his probation for a robbery offense would be revoked because of the traffic violation, King led the CHP on a high-speed chase, eventually hitting 115 miles per hour, according to the police. By the time he was caught and ordered to exit his vehicle, several L.A.P.D. squad cars had arrived on the scene. A struggle ensued, and some of the officers quickly decided that King was resisting arrest. Sergeant Stacey Koon fired two shots into King with a TASER gun, and after that failed to subdue him, the officers, including Laurence Powell, beat him mercilessly with their batons.*

Certainly, nobody would advocate for police officers randomly beating a citizen. In this instance though, after a high-speed car chase that put lives at risk, non-compliance with officers, failure of the taser to have effect (usually a sign of someone on drugs), police could have justified shooting him. They didn't.

If Ms. Waters wants to use the words "Righteous anger", it would be better applied to these officers operating under high stress.

"It's time for the bully pulpit of the White House to bring the gangstas in, put them around the table and let them know that if they don't come up with loan modifications and keep people in their homes that they've worked so hard for, we're gonna tax them out of business." **(Maxine Waters)**

It is unclear why Ms. Waters would want to bring "gangstas" into the White House, but she must have had her reasons.

It appears she is upset about people losing their homes. She does not seem to realize why people were losing their homes and the role she herself played in the housing market collapse.

Maxine Waters was co-sponsor of the Community Reinvestment Act (CRA) Modernization Act. This act forced banks to make mortgage loans to people who the banks knew would be unlikely to pay it off in the end. Individual bankers were even rewarded with kickbacks for making these loans.

According to Bader, Hans,2008, *The current mortgage crisis came about in large part because of Clinton-era government pressure on lenders to make risky loans to make homeownership more affordable for lower-income Americans and those with a poor credit history. Those steps encouraged riskier mortgage lending by minimizing the role of credit histories in lending decisions, loosening required debt-to-equity ratios to allow borrowers to make small or even no down payments at all, and encouraging lenders the use of floating or adjustable interest-rate mortgages, including those with low teasers.*

Clinton Administration Housing Secretary Andrew Cuomo helped spawn the mortgage crisis through his pressure on lenders to promote affordable housing and diversity. Andrew Cuomo, the youngest Housing and Urban Development Secretary in history, made a series of decisions between 1997 and 2001 that gave birth to the country's housing crisis. He took actions that, in combination with many other factors, helped plunge Fannie and Freddie into the subprime markets without putting in place the means to monitor their increasingly risky investments.

Cuomo turned the Federal Housing Administration mortgage program into a sweetheart lender with sky-high loan ceilings and no money down, and he legalized what a federal judge has branded kickbacks to brokers that have fueled the sale of

Ms. Waters also seems to be threatening to tax the banks out of business if they do not make loan modifications. Her comments could easily be construed as extortion. Of course, Ms. Waters could never carry through with the threat because she obviously does not understand that banks do not pay taxes.

Job Description for U.S. Representative: As a House member you represent a certain district in your state. This means that you will stay in touch with your constituents and, hence, you will be more aware of their opinions and needs and be able to advocate for them in Washington. Also, one of your major job duties will be to raise revenue through taxes. Further, you will participate in committees to study bills, hold public hearings, get expert testimony, and listen to voters so that legislation can be passed. Further, you might serve on a joint committee with Senate members.

Being offended by the President is not her job. "Educating" people on who she thinks he is, is also not her job. "Educating" people on the dangers she thinks he poses to the country, is still not her job. "Exposing" the President is not her job.

A U.S. Representative has important work, but none of what she listed is her job.

"If Hillary Clinton had won the White House, I believe that given what Comey did to her, and what he tried to do, she should have fired him." **(Maxine Waters)**

Hillary did not win the White House, so Waters' comment is superfluous. If Clinton had won, then whatever Waters is claiming Comey did to Clinton would not have occurred, so why would Clinton fire him?

If Hillary had been elected, it would be hard for her to justify firing Comey because she was elected and there would be no damage to her from Comey's actions.

In Reality, Comey was Clintons best friend during her investigation. If anyone else was being investigated and have had as much evidence of wrong-doing as she did, they would be in jail.

It is now well known that Comey had no intention of seeking prosecution against Hillary Clinton. He had even prepared his written decision prior to her, or other key witnesses being questioned.

Waters claim that Clinton should have fired Comey if she had been elected makes very little sense. It did, however make sense for President Trump to fire Comey.

President Trump did fire Comey. It should be expected that Maxine Waters would be happy that he was fire. But, no.

According to Vespa, Matt, 2017, *Rep. Maxine Waters is still on the warpath. She wants to impeach Trump, and has said that she will fight every day to make that happen. She has said he has no business being president (sorry, that's how elections work). She called the president a disgusting, poor excuse of a man. One of the benefits of being a California Democrat is you can just be stark raving mad all the time, say insane things, and be shamelessly hypocritical with no political consequences. In January, Waters was visibly irate with then-FBI Director James Comey. Now that he's out, you would think she's overjoyed. Nope. She's not because Trump fired Mr. Comey and not Hillary. It's a level of hypocrisy that initially drew confusion from NBC's Peter Alexander.*

PETER ALEXANDER: So, Congresswoman, respecting that be to be clear, you believe it would have been better to keep in place an FBI Director who you said had no credibility to oversee this investigation than to find someone who you think would be a better choice.

MAXINE WATERS: No. But I believe the president thought that. Don't forget. You're talking about what some Democrats said, what I said, but don't forget. He was the president. The president supported him. He had confidence in him. It was within his power.

ALEXANDER: But you said he had no credibility, so it would make sense that he get rid of him.

WATERS: No, no, no. Under investigation. This president basically has interfered with an investigation where he may be implicated. That's outrageous. And that's why we're having so much of a conversation about it today. Everybody is talking about it because this is highly unusual.

ALEXANDER: The bottom line is you think an FBI director without credibility would have been best served in this position to try to pursue this investigation.

WATERS: I think that if the president would have fired him when he first came in, he would not have to be in a position now where he is trying to make up a story about why. It does not meet the smell test.

ALEXANDER: Understood. So, if Hillary Clinton had won the White House, would you have recommended that she fire FBI Director James Comey?

WATERS: Well, let me tell you something. If she had won the White House, I believe that given what he did to her, and what he tried to do, she should have fired him. Yes.

ALEXANDER: So, she should have fired him, but he shouldn't fire him. This is why I'm confused.

WATERS: No, you're not confused. If the president is implicated in an investigation --

ALEXANDER: I am confused.

Some people cannot be happy even when they get what they wished for.

"We do not have a crisis at Freddie Mac, and particularly Fannie Mae, under the outstanding leadership of Frank Raines." **(Maxine Waters)**

Waters obviously has a fondness for Raines that transcends his leadership skills. Raines has had his share of issues accounting for money.

Franklin Delano "Frank" Raines was an American business executive. He is the former CEO of Fannie Mae, and served as White House budget director under President Bill Clinton. His role leading Fannie Mae has come under scrutiny. He has been called one of the 25 People to Blame for the Financial Crisis by Time magazine.

On December 21, 2004, Raines accepted what he called "early retirement" from his position as CEO while U.S. Securities and Exchange Commission continued to investigate accounting irregularities. He was accused by The Office of Federal Housing Enterprise Oversight (OFHEO) of abetting widespread accounting errors, which included the shifting of losses so senior executives, such as himself, could earn large bonuses.

In 2006, the OFHEO announced a suit against Raines to recover the $90 million in payments made to Raines based on the overstated earnings, initially estimated to be $9 billion but had been announced as $6.3 billion.

Civil charges were filed against Raines and two other former executives in which the OFHEO sought $110 million in penalties and $115 million in returned bonuses from the three accused. On April 18, 2008, the government announced a settlement with Raines and the other two executives. The three agreed to the payment of fines totaling about $3 million, which were paid by Fannie's insurance policies. Raines also agreed to donate to charity the proceeds from the sale of $1.8 million of his Fannie stock newly issued to him by the company and to give up stock options, which were valued at $15.6 million when issued.

The stock options however had no value. The OFHEO press release said Raines also gave up an estimated $5.3 million of "other benefits" said to be related to his pension and forgone bonuses. Raines denied that he gave up any such benefits or paid any money out of pocket for the settlement.

The Wall Street Journal called it a paltry settlement which allowed Raines and the other two executives to keep the bulk of their riches. In 2003 alone, Raines's compensation was over $20 million.

Given Ms. Waters questionable financial activities, perhaps she considered Frank Raines to be her mentor. In any case, there was a major financial crisis under the leadership of Frank Raines; the mortgage crisis that caused millions to lose their homes.

"I think that when you saw Donald Trump absolutely calling Hillary Clinton crooked, the "lock her up, lock her up," all of that was developed. I think that was developed strategically with people from the Kremlin, with Vladimir Putin." (**Maxine Waters**)

There is no evidence now, nor was there then that the Russians strategically developed a plan for Trump supporters to chant "lock her up".

Trump was an unknown factor to the Russians. They likely supported Hillary Clinton because they knew she could be bribed, they had already bribed her.

Trump supporters were mostly tired of corruption in Washington and the elite getting away with corruption. Hillary Clinton, like Maxine Waters, is a poster child for corruption. Many are still hopeful that Hillary Clinton will someday be held accountable for her crimes.

Waters has been the Democrats voice to impeach President Trump. Her piercing cries for impeachment began before the inauguration and continue today. She becomes irritated when she is asked what basis there is for the President to be impeached and she is unable to provide a coherent response.

In responding Waters once urged the crowd not to get hung up on what law to invoke in the impeachment process:

Impeachment is about whatever the Congress says it is. There is no law that dictates impeachment. What the Constitution says is high crimes and misdemeanors, and we define that. (Maxine Waters)

She was basically admitting that there was no real basis for impeachment, but she will keep looking, and whatever she discovers (or creates) she will try to make stick.

Ms. Waters certainly knows the word impeachment, but it is less certain she understands the process.

Impeachment is the process by which a legislative body formally levels charges against a high official of government. Impeachment does not necessarily mean removal from office; it is only a formal statement of charges, akin to an indictment in criminal law, and is only the first step towards removal.

Once an individual is impeached, he or she must then face the possibility of conviction via legislative vote, which then entails the removal of the individual from office.

Because impeachment and conviction of officials involve an overturning of the normal constitutional procedures by which individuals achieve high office (election, ratification, or appointment) and because it generally requires a supermajority, they are usually reserved for those deemed to have committed serious abuses of their office.

In the United States, for example, impeachment at the federal level is limited to those who may have committed high crimes and misdemeanors.

The charge of high crimes and misdemeanors covers allegations of misconduct peculiar to officials, such as perjury, abuse of authority, bribery, intimidation, misuse of assets, failure to supervise, dereliction of duty, conduct unbecoming, and refusal to obey a lawful order.

If Hillary Clinton had been elected, every single one of the high crimes listed above would have applied. Donald Trump, not so much.

Ms. Waters, impeachment is not whatever you or congress decide it is. The American voters elected President Trump, and you cannot arbitrarily go against the American voters.

"If [Donald Trump] wants to do good things, let's see it. Let him do it. I can't stop him from doing good things." (**Maxine Waters**)

It is true that Maxine Waters cannot stop President Trump from doing good things. The bigger question is why would she want to stop him from doing good things?

What she can and does do is put a negative spin on everything he tries to do and obstruct him from getting good things accomplished. She simply makes things more difficult. Even if it is something she has called for, such as firing James Comey, she will oppose it simply to disparage the presidency.

She is constantly calling for the President's impeachment, even though she cannot list a simple impeachable offense he allegedly perpetrated.

Her concept of good things is different than the President's and many of the American people. Having the government take over private businesses, taxing banks, removing farm subsidies and keeping Obamacare ,which is killing the middle class and small businesses, are her ideas of good things.

"You cannot be successful and continue to be a victim." **(Maxine Waters)**

This comment is hypocrisy at its finest. Democratic party members are well known for doing something wrong, denying wrong-doing, getting caught, blaming someone else and eventually portraying themselves as victims. This pattern is so predictable, Americans wait for each step, knowing where it will eventually end up.

Hillary Clinton portrays herself as a victim. She blames everyone for her election loss except herself and her inner circle, which is exactly where the blame belongs.

Maxine Waters is a classic example of this as well. After an I interview that could be considered a tirade against the President, Ms. Waters once again played the victim card.

"They're trying every way they can to discredit me, or to make people uncomfortable with me, all of that. So, you're gonna be hearing a lot more from them these people who are all, you know, aligned around trying to discredit Maxine Waters because she has stayed on Trump's case so much," **(Maxine Waters)**

Waters has said unhinged, incoherent stuff for years. If Waters wants to know who is discrediting her, all she must do is look in the mirror.

"And so, you're going to hear a lot more from them," she added. "Don't believe anything they're saying." (Maxine Waters)

Perhaps it is paranoia on her part. The President and Republicans do not really seem to be saying anything about Ms. Waters. After dealing with her in congress for so many years, I am sure they know it is best to ignore her and her ramblings and move on. She believes she is more important than she really is. She has already been scrutinized by political rivals during her corruption hearings. Otherwise she is tolerated and ignored.

She is right though that people who view themselves as victims do not make good leaders.

"Others say that that's not good for the country [to resist Donald's Trump] and that they should

work with this new administration on policies...”
(Maxine Waters)

Few in congress can say that they agree with every President on every policy. If that were the case, there would be no need to have a congress.

Resisting a person because you may not like them while ignoring the work that the American people hired you to do is not good for the country. No sane person could argue to the contrary.

As an adult, you learn to collaborate with others, even some you may not like. As a member of congress, it is you job and duty to move beyond petty differences and get the job done. Nobody is going to give you a participation medal for obstructing the President and the other members of congress who want to get things done.

“I am not afraid of anybody. This is a tough game. You can't be intimidated. You can't be

frightened. And as far as I'm concerned, the Tea Party can go straight to hell." **(Maxine Waters)**

Fear is a primal emotion that helps our decisions. Fear helps us understand the potential consequences of decisions. Fear motivates us to protect our country from enemies, domestic and foreign.

Chess is a tough game. Being a member of congress is a job, not a game. The job can be tough at times. As a member of congress, you must work with people who have differing visions for America. You also represent all people, not just a select group that agree with you. Decisions must be based on the common good of all, even if it conflicts with your own personal agenda.

Ms. Waters has condemned a whole group of voters to Hell. Elected officials do not do this, they see value in all and listen to all. They don't just listen to the squeaking hamster wheel inside their own head.

"I don't see white police officers slamming the heads of little white boys into police cars."
(Maxine Waters)

Ms. Waters lives outside of her crime ridden district in a very affluent neighborhood that has very little crime. It is doubtful that she has personally witnessed police activities other than what is portrayed in the media.

Police have a strict set of policies for when physical interaction can occur and at what level. The level is to match the threat. Police are humans and as such mistakes can happen. They can perceive an elevated threat when none exists, and when that happens they are held accountable.

The inference in Ms. Waters comment is that little black boys routinely have their heads slammed into police cars. She would need to clarify this contention for an appropriate response to be made. There are no media reports of little black boys having heads slammed against police cars.

The media shows a skewed representation of crime in America. They often focus on violence by whites against blacks. It suggests that there is an enormous problem with whites attacking blacks. This is not the reality.

The Department of Justice (DOJ) collects statistics from law agencies throughout the country. The number statistics show several interesting facts. 94% of black people who are murdered, are murdered by other black people. 87% of white people who are murdered are murdered by other white people. There are 5 times as many white people killed by black people (320,000) per year as there are blacks killed by whites (63,000). There are 25 times as many violent crimes (crimes that could result in death) committed by black people than white people.

The statistics show that deaths caused by the police breakdown to 13% Black, 17% Hispanic, 63% White and 7% Other.

One of the reasons these statistics are created is to ensure those in powerful positions have the facts needed to make educated decisions. Making decisions on false portrayals in the media would be unconscionable.

Ms. Waters would be well served by using these statistics. The country would be well served if somebody puts these statistics in an audio book format for Ms. Waters.

"I have a right to my anger, and I don't want anybody telling me I shouldn't be, that it's not nice to be, and that something's wrong with me because I get angry." **(Maxine Waters)**

Maxine Waters is well known for her anger which comes through in many of her interactions. It has earned her the nick name Mad Maxine. Her quote suggests that she embraces her anger.

Waters however made another comment describing the effect of anger.

"When people are angry and enraged, they do senseless things." (Maxine Waters)

If both of her contentions are correct, it explains her congressional record perfectly, anger followed by doing senseless things.

"I've been in this struggle for many years now. I understand racism. I understand that there are a lot of people in this country who don't care about the problems of the inner city. We have to fight every day that we get up for every little thing that we get. And so, I keep struggling." (Maxine Waters)

Ms. Waters doesn't fight for every little thing she gets, nor does she struggle. She is wealthy. She lives in a 4.5-million-dollar mansion in an affluent neighborhood far from her poor constituents. Pretending she shares their struggle is non-sensical.

She has been in office for over 30 years and little improvement has occurred in her district. Crime is higher in her district than almost anywhere in the country.

"Every time I've talked about impeachment, I've said we've got to connect the dots, we've got to get the facts, we've got to do the investigation. That is what leads to impeachment and I also said that Donald Trump will lead us right there." (Maxine Waters)

That's not how impeachment works, but have fun.

"President Trump basically has interfered with an investigation where he may be implicated. That's outrageous. And that's why we're having so much of a conversation about it today. Everybody is talking about it because this is highly unusual." **(Maxine Waters)**

According to McLaughlin, Dan, 2017, *There are a number of important takeaways from today's Comey hearings, but one of the big ones elaborated on a point I hit yesterday in discussing Comey's prepared statement: Trump was never under FBI investigation during the time that Comey headed the FBI, Comey personally told Trump that three times, and Trump grew increasingly frustrated that Comey wouldn't clear the "cloud" over his head by publicly saying so. Indeed, Trump's explanation to Lester Holt of why he fired Comey is entirely consistent with this. But with Comey's repeated and emphatic testimony that Trump was not under investigation, we have some new revisionist history: wildly backtracking liberals and Democrats claiming that nobody ever said Trump was under FBI investigation. And this is simply untrue. Here's a sampling of what Democrats, liberals, and the media were saying back when Comey was privately reassuring Trump that he wasn't under investigation.*

Donald Trump had good reasons to fire James Comey. The American people, by and large, approved of his decision. Maxine Waters had recommended that had Hillary Clinton won the election that she should fire Comey because in her words, Comey had no credibility.

According to Glum, Julia, 2017, these are the reasons President Trump had to fire Comey.

He hurt the FBI's reputation

A memorandum prepared by Deputy Attorney General Rod Rosenstein recommending Comey's termination kicks off with the fact that over the past year ... the FBI's reputation and credibility have suffered substantial damage, and it has affected the entire Department of Justice. He mishandled the Clinton email investigation.

Rosenstein writes that Comey should not have given a news conference last July recommending that Clinton, who used a private email server while Secretary of State, not face criminal charges. The Deputy Attorney General writes that Comey should have turned his findings over to federal prosecutors. He also takes issue with Comey's decision to send a letter just days before the November election revealing newly discovered Clinton emails. When federal agents and prosecutors quietly open a criminal investigation, we are not concealing anything; we are simply following the longstanding policy that we refrain from publicizing non-public information.

It was not appropriate for the FBI Director to make any recommendation to the Department of Justice (DOJ) on whether to prosecute Hillary Clinton. It is now apparent that the DOJ had orchestrated the investigation and the predetermined results. Comey's announcing that the case had been re-opened may have had an impact on the few voters who had not decided by that point. In general, though, this election was bi-polar and few people were undecided at the time of Comey's announcement.

He broke with tradition

Rosenstein cites several attorneys general and other authorities who decried Comey's actions as a departure from the department's widely respected, nonpartisan traditions. Rosenstein writes that we should reject the departure and return to the traditions.

James Comey was in an untenable position. If he went against Lynch and Obama mandates on the investigation, he would be fired. If Hillary Clinton had won the election, she likely would have had the same inclination as Waters and fired Comey. As more information has come out, it became apparent that Comey mishandled the investigation, even creating a letter exonerating Clinton weeks before he interviewed her and other key witnesses.

Trump doesn't trust him

By October, when he was bringing attention to a new cache of Clinton emails, Trump loved him, but in November, when Comey said he hadn't found material that justified charges, the pendulum had swung again. You can't review 650,000 new emails in eight days. You can't do it, folks, Trump said at a rally. Hillary Clinton is guilty. She knows it, the FBI knows it, the people know it.

Despite Comey's recommendation, he had tough criticisms of Clinton's handling of e-mails and confidential information. If this had been anyone else in government, or the military, they would be in jail. It was clear someone was pressuring Comey to end the investigation. The President is correct that the 650,000 could not *possibly have been reviewed in eight days, given how long it took to review the initial 50,000.*

Trump is embarrassed by him

The president recently accused his predecessor, Barack Obama, of wiretapping his phones during the campaign. Comey has shut down this allegation, explaining that Obama could not order a wiretap of anyone's phone unchecked. I have no information that supports those tweets, and we have looked carefully inside the FBI, Comey said in March. The Department of Justice has asked me to share with you that the answer is the same for the Department of Justice and all its components. The department has no information that supports those tweets.

It has since been validated that Trumps contention that Trump Tower had been wire tapped (placed under surveillance) was correct.

*"**Some are arguing that the Democrats should resist at every turn [to Donald's Trump administration], and some Democrats are saying that's the strategy that Democrats should now employ.**" (**Maxine Waters**)*

According to the Mayo Clinic, 2015, *You're shopping with your toddler in a busy department store. He or she has spied a toy that you don't intend to buy. Suddenly you're at the center of a gale-force temper tantrum. Everyone is looking at you. The goal is to embarrass you and prevent you from continuing being productive.*

A tantrum is the expression of a young child's frustration with the challenges of the moment. Perhaps your child is having trouble figuring something out or completing a specific task. Maybe your child doesn't have the vocabulary or can't find the words to express his or her feelings. Frustration might trigger anger, resulting in a temper tantrum.

Young children don't plan to frustrate or embarrass their parents. For most toddlers, tantrums are a way to express frustration. For older children, tantrums might be a learned behavior. If you reward tantrums with something your child wants, or you

As painful as it is to watch, this is precisely the behavior strategy our Democrat leaders are engaging in. Obviously, this is a learned behavior that has been reinforced in the past.

It is sad because these are not children. They are adults. They are our leaders. They continue to do anything they can to embarrass the President. They insult his family, insult his voter base, insult his cabinet, and insult him.

It is perplexing to watch people over 70 throw a tantrum. As adults, we realize they are only embarrassing themselves.

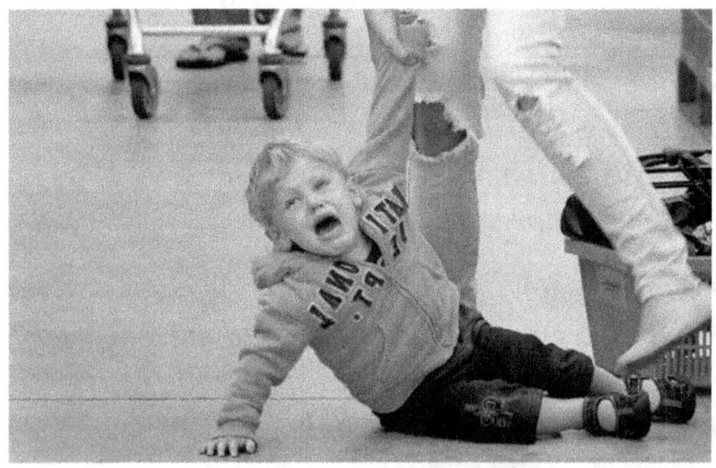

These tantrums are planned, not spontaneous. In fact, Ms. Waters' quote suggests it does not matter what the President proposes, the Democrats plan to oppose.

It is understandable that the Democrats are frustrated. They certainly had expected Hillary Clinton to win and were prepared for her coronation. Clinton lost, and suddenly the wonderful world of democrats collapsed. Democrats found themselves in the minority in both the senate and house. Their power to harm America was gone. All they had left was to obstruct, tantrum, embarrass others and portray themselves as victims.

Our elected officials are supposed to be mature adults who understand nobody gets everything they want. They not doing their job and preventing others from doing their work on behalf of the American people.

"I just think the American people had better understand what's going on. This is a bunch of scumbags. That's what [Russians] are!" **(Maxine Waters)**

The U.S. Constitution parcels out foreign relations powers to both the executive and legislative branches. It grants some powers, like command of the military, exclusively to the President and others, like the regulation of foreign commerce, to Congress, while still others it divides among the two or simply does not assign.

A U.S. Representative is a public figure and will be under scrutiny for past, present and future actions. Ms. Waters is known for speaking without thinking. This quality is dangerous when it comes to international relationships. Imagine her fury if President Trump made Waters' "scumbag" comment about Mexicans, or Kenyans, or even Russians.

Thankfully, the Russians do not take Maxine Waters any more seriously than Americans do.

"The shouting, the overrunning of the Capitol, the sneaking in of Tea Party participants into the basement of the Capitol, the name-calling, the spitting, all of that.... The Tea Party emerges as not only outrageous, but they have turned up the volume in ways that even Code Pink have not been able to do." (**Maxine Waters**)

Maxine Waters hates the Tea Party nearly as much as she hates the President. Waters, like most democrats, believe taxes should be raised to meet the budget. Republicans tend to keep the status quo or a reduce taxes. The Tea Party advocates for deep tax cuts.

Her contempt for the Tea Party was enhanced when a group decided to confront Waters at a Town Hall meeting in her district. Waters was caught off guard since most people who live in her district do not want to be there. It was incomprehensible to her that Tea Party members would come to South Central to confront her. Keep in mind, Waters lives a significant distance from her constituents, so obviously she doesn't really want to be there either.

Waters was also greeted by "poverty pimp" posters of herself throughout her journey. This was new for Waters. She was not used to people protesting her. She had been spared mainly because nobody took her seriously. But now that she was a self -proclaimed warrior against the President she became a fair target. She was flustered during her Town Hall meeting and less coherent than usual. She left the meeting and headed to her mansion in an affluent area of Los Angeles seeking solace. When she arrived, she found protesters in front of her home as well. She then declared war on the Tea Party.

Waters was not a stranger to protests because she has participated in protests alongside nefarious groups.

Ms. Waters advocates for the right of people to protest provided they agree with her. She had conviction when people who disagreed with and protested her.

If Ms. Waters continues to inject herself into the limelight by denigrating the President and his followers, she will continue to have to listen to those who oppose her as well.

"The most upsetting part of the new administration is discovering that the person who won the election and became the president of the United States of America is a man who has no good values. His character astounds me. I can't believe that we have a president who would lie, who would distort, and who does not appear to have an appreciation for government and how it works." **(Maxine Waters)**

Ms. Waters is practiced in the art of both ambiguity and deflection. She makes vague claims of character flaws in others, that she can later distance herself from if popular opinion turns against her. She has been in office for almost 40 years and you should expect that significant positive change has occurred for people in her district.

According to Malkin, M. 2017, *Waters has spent 37 years in office, many of those years as head of the Congressional Black Caucus, promising to make life better for constituents in economically ravaged South-Central Los Angeles. What do the denizens of her district have to show for it? Staggering levels of persistent unemployment, poverty, and gang violence as the 25th anniversary of the L.A. riots looms this coming weekend. What does Representative Waters have to show for it?*

She's earned a lifetime of left-wing adoration for whitewashing the deadly riots as a "rebellion," excusing the week-long shooting, (which resulted in 53 deaths, 4000 injured, over a billion dollars in damage, and loss of the community hub) looting, and arson orgy as a spontaneous reaction to a lot of injustice and a lot of alienation and frustration, and coddling Crips and Bloods gang members, with whom she performed the Electric Slide as part of her fearless support and understanding of young people and their efforts at self-expression.

Her federally funded Maxine Waters Employment Preparation Center was a gang-infested boondoggle. She embraced Damian Williams, the infamous thug who hurled a chunk of concrete at white truck driver Reginald Denny and performed a victory dance over the bloodied innocent bystander. And Waters and her family personally profited from her rise to racially demagogic power.

Donald Trump has been in politics less than a year. His brief time in office has had a tremendous positive impact on the economy. The stock market is soaring and over a million new jobs have been created. Government spending has been frozen, and waste has been cut in every department. Unemployment and fuel costs are down. The National debt has been reduced. Nearly a trillion dollars in waste and mismanagement has been identified and recovered. Illegal immigration is down 70% and ISIS forces have been defeated in Raqqa. He has demonstrated extreme competence despite unwarranted obstruction by those on the left, including Ms. Waters.

As a private citizen, Mr. Trump quietly helped others.

According to Charter, Justen, 2015, Since Donald Trump announced he was running for president, he has seen no shortage of the media spotlight. But one thing that fails to receive coverage: how Trump has touched the lives of others. Here are 5 acts of kindness that reveal there's more to the billionaire than just his big celebrity persona.

The time he gave sanctuary to Grammy Award winning singer Jennifer Hudson after three of her family members were murdered: *When Hudson's mother, brother and nephew were gunned down in Chicago, she put everything on hold for a while. She stayed at Trump Tower to grieve, where Donald Trump didn't charge her a dime and* *provided security for her and a few of her family members.*

Airlines wouldn't accommodate a boy who had serious medical issues, so Trump offered his jet to help: *Three-year-old Andrew Ten needed to go to New York to receive some special medical attention. But there was one big problem. The airlines refused to board him because Ten required several different pieces of medical equipment on the flight. Ten's parents put in a call to Trump, who then dispatched his private jet to meet their pressing needs.*

Ten's father said Trump is a good man. He has three children of his own and he knows what being a parent is all about.

He helped save a family's working farm that was going into foreclosure: *In 1986, Annabell Hill was in danger of losing her family farm. On top of that, her husband had just committed suicide hoping that his life insurance policy would cover the remaining balance that they owed. When Trump saw her tragic story, he decided to do something about it.*

According to the New York Times, Donald Trump, the New York real estate tycoon, helped prevent foreclosure on the family farm whose owner had committed suicide to try to save his land.

Mrs. Hill proposed to bank officials that the land be sold privately so she could keep some of the 705 acres. Parts of the farm have been in the Hill family for three generations.

After Sergeant Andrew Tahmooressi was released from a prison in Mexico, The Donald sent him a big check to help get him back on his feet: *Tahmooressi spent seven months in a Mexican prison. During that time, he was beaten and even chained to a bed. When he was released, Trump sent him a check for twenty-five thousand dollars.*

What Trump did for a bus driver who helped save a woman from jumping off a bridge: *Darnell Barton was driving his bus across a bridge when he spotted a woman on the other side of railing, staring down at the traffic below. Barton stopped the bus and approached the woman. After one of his passengers explained they didn't want to see someone die, Barton managed to put his arm around her and the would be jumper agreed to come to the other side of the bridge.*

After hearing about what Barton did, Trump sent him ten thousand dollars.

Trump said he thought that Barton's intervention was beautiful to see. He thought Barton was a great guy with an amazing heart and should be rewarded.

Clearly, Donald Trump isn't just a good businessman, he's a Good Samaritan, too.

"Black women are going to have to take more leadership. I think we are prepared because we bring a tenaciousness with us. We do not fear losing friends, allies, or jobs." (Maxine Waters)

Ms. Waters is correct in saying more black women need to take leadership roles. She is also correct in the tenacity of black women and the power they hold and could bring to our country. If there is one redeeming quality for Maxine Waters, it is that she has opened the doors for others; more competent and educated black women to follow in her footsteps. She inspired an under-represented population to aspire to do greater things.

Continuing her comment, she digressed into dark territory. She claims black women are not afraid to lose friends, allies, and jobs. Most people realize that jobs are an essential part of being empowered and not controlled by government assistance. Friends are what makes our lives enjoyable. Allies are essential for anyone in politics if they wish to accomplish anything for the American people.

It's hard to imagine anybody would relish the idea of losing jobs, friends, and allies. For most people these are essential parts of life.

"All of these people who are organized with these oil-and-gas interests, that's in the administration and friends of the President of the United States [Donald Trump], these back channeling that you see. These are a bunch of scumbags. That's what they are." **(Maxine Waters)**

The irony of Maxine Waters' comments may be lost on her. She represents an area of Los Angeles. Los Angeles was built through a collaboration of the oil and automobile industries. One of the largest urban oil fields in the country is in Inglewood, which is part of Ms. Waters' district.

According to Mehta, Jonaki, and Sonari Glinton, 2016, *Throughout Los Angeles, oil is hidden in plain sight. Even Los Angelenos sometimes forget it is there, often with active pumps hidden in windowless buildings. J. Paul Getty or Edward Doheny, men who made their fortunes on oil and then made LA.*

Los Angeles is a world center for transportation, fashion, manufacturing, and entertainment. In the heart of this metropolis, oil is hidden in plain sight. If you go on a walk to clear your head at NPR's Culver City studios, cross the street and you're in one of the largest producing urban oil fields in America.

When people think about Los Angeles, they tend to think of big skyscrapers and beaches. they don't generally tend to think of oil wells.

This is fairly valuable real estate, with some rather expensive homes close by the Inglewood oil field. Baldwin Hills and View Park neighborhoods are considered the "Black Beverly Hills" for former residents such as Tina Turner, Ray Charles and Nancy Wilson. "This oil is clearly very valuable to justify using that space for those oil pumps.

It's the oil wells that made modern life in LA possible. The LA Basin is very isolated and vast. That makes getting goods into the area difficult, and it made transporting goods around the region very tough. That is until the invention of the automobile and the discovery of oil.

You can find oil wells hidden all over Los Angeles. Beverly Hills High School has multiple oil wells on its campus. Edward Doheny, for whom the major thoroughfare in Beverly Hills is named, discovered oil under a private residence in 1892. His find set off an oil-drilling spree.

Part of what made Los Angeles oil so attractive, was that the oil was close to the surface and easy to extract. Add to that the newly invented automobile, incredible weather, and a port, and that's a recipe for exponential expansion. Without oil there would be no modern Los Angeles. The petroleum industry of course made it possible to have Hollywood. It made it made it possible to build an infrastructure to transport agricultural produce from other areas to help support the growth of a relatively large city very quickly.

It's difficult to overstate just how much oil was being produced in LA back in the 1920s.The production from here made Los Angeles the equivalent of Saudi Arabia today.

In the county of Los Angeles, more than 17,000 people are employed in oil and gas extraction, while an additional 12,000 people work at gas stations, the report said. The industry generates about $5.7 million in labor income.

California enjoyed $21.6 billion in state and local tax revenues from gas and oil production. These energy sectors also created a combined 468,000 direct and indirect jobs.

Despite the oil industry creating her city, and its continuing finances keeping the California economy from collapsing, and the near half million jobs the industry creates, Waters deems those who work in the oil industry as "scumbags". Nonsensical.

"Take a look at the way that Trump has described some of the foreign countries that we deal with - some that are allies and some that are not. China is one example. He said they were currency manipulators, but after he sat down with President Xi and had a piece of chocolate cake, he then said they were no longer currency manipulators." **(Maxine Waters)**

Currency manipulation is not an easy thing to understand. The relationship between two currencies can alter the value of negotiated trade agreements benefiting one side over the other. There are internal and external implications to the buying power of a given currency.

According to Wolff, Alan, 2015, *With the sudden depreciation of China's renminbi, it's worth looking at the link between currency values and trade agreements. China's currency last week dropped by a cumulative 4.4% against the U.S. dollar, making Chinese exports cheaper and imports into China more expensive by that amount.*

The effect on trade can be substantial. With the U.S. average tariff on industrial goods well under 2%, this change in China's currency value easily swamps most U.S. tariffs. And given the fact that the U.S. dollar was already strong, this move is an added disadvantage to U.S. exports headed for China compared to exports from other countries.

Between 2000 and 2014, China definitely manipulated its currency. Once Chinese President Xi took power, the practice had stopped. Trump was correct it had happened and was also correct in his statement that it was no longer occurring. Presidents Bush and Obama should have addressed the matter during their terms but did not.

The War on Poverty is the unofficial name for legislation first introduced by United States President Lyndon B. Johnson during his State of the Union address on January 8, 1964. Johnson proposed this legislation in response to a national poverty rate of around nineteen percent.

The popularity of a war on poverty waned after the 1960s. Deregulation, growing criticism of the welfare state, and an ideological shift to reducing federal aid to impoverished people in the 1980s and 1990s culminated in the Personal Responsibility and Work Opportunity Act (WOA) of 1996, which President Bill Clinton claimed, ended welfare as we know it. The WOA was one of Bill Clinton's best accomplishments. Instead of handouts and people relying on the charity of the government, it provided people a chance to provide services in exchange for help. It gave people an opportunity to become a productive part of society.

There is no reason that people who can work receive government money. Welfare is meant for people who cannot work or somehow cannot find work. The Opportunity Act allowed for worker training, internships, or direct volunteer services. The community was to get something out of the money the government put into helping others. It was designed to build personal responsibility and decrease future dependence on government handouts.

Maxine Waters voted against the Workers Opportunity Act.

By keeping her constituent's dependent upon the government, she was giving herself job security.

"On Immigration policy and reform [Republicans] are on the wrong side of the track. ... They would have you believe that if they get into office, they are going to make sure that they are going to get rid of everyone in our society who was not born in America." (**Maxine Waters**)

Illegal immigrants and legal immigrants are as different as a potato and a rock. Explaining this to liberals is like talking to a wall. President Trump is married to a legal immigrant, as is Jeb Bush. Nobody on either side of the aisle has suggested revoking citizenship of everyone in our society who was not born in America. Legal immigrants are U.S. citizens and are afforded all the rights as other American citizens.

It is widely accepted by both sides of the aisle that most illegal immigrants are here for economic reasons, or to escape violent crime in their own countries. Once here they do not enjoy the protections granted by U.S. labor laws. They are unlikely to report crimes against them to police. They are at high risk of being exploited by employers and others.

Democrats are bringing in slave labor for themselves and their rich friends. Hollywood types will have cheap baby sitters, gardeners, maids, and vulnerable women looking for jobs for their sponsors to sexually harass and exploit.

Democrats always pretend that they're bringing in illegal immigrants because they care about people. If they cared about people, they would start by caring about the plight of fellow citizens who are living in poverty.

Democrats are exploiting poverty both in this country and outside this country, for their own selfish benefits when they lie to their followers that they like illegal immigrants. Illegal immigrants have no way to work legally in the United States which means they can only work for slave wages for masters who will keep them silent with threats of deportation.

Part of the fortune of Nancy Pelosi, defender of the working man, is a Napa Valley vineyard worth $25 million that she owns with her husband. The vineyard produces expensive grapes for high-end wines. Napa grapes bring up to $4,000 a ton compared with $300 a ton for, say, San Joaquin grapes.

But Pelosi, winner of the 2003 Cesar Chavez award from the United Farm Workers, hires only nonunion workers and sells these grapes to nonunion wineries.

Pelosi's steadfast opposition to any attempts to enhance border security and stem the flow of illegal immigration into the U.S. becomes all the more interesting since she is among rich employers who financially benefit from cheap foreign labor.

Pelosi has not been a fan of employer sanctions against the hiring of illegal aliens. In 2003, she accused immigration officers of conducting raids on Wal-Mart stores that led to the arrest of more than 300 illegal aliens.

Half of the migrant labor force in the Napa Valley consisted of undocumented workers, without whom not one bottle of wine would get made there.

While most illegal immigrants are here to better their lives, others are criminals escaping their country and taking advantage of the poorly enforced immigration laws. Law enforcement is hindered by so-called sanctuary cities which refuse to turn illegal immigrants accused of crimes over to the federal enforcement agencies.

According to Lucas, Ryan, 2017, Los Angeles sued the Justice Department over the Trump administration's threat to cut millions in federal funding for so-called sanctuary cities, which limit their cooperation with federal authorities on immigration enforcement.

The lawsuit seeks to join similar legal challenges that the state of California and the city of San Francisco lodged earlier this month against the department over new conditions it has imposed on federal grants for local law enforcement. The city of Chicago is also suing the department over the matter in a separate suit.

The legal claims all accuse the Trump administration of threatening to withhold funding to try to force local jurisdictions to enforce federal immigration laws. The administration would place L.A. with the untenable choice of risking a key public safety grant.

Since 2014, violent crime has risen in Los Angeles. That's why it is so baffling that the city would challenge policies designed to keep residents of L.A. safer, especially from the scourge of transnational gang activity from MS-13, 18th Street Gang and others.

Reversing sanctuary city policies is about more than just enforcing federal immigration law by detaining criminals here illegally, it's about re-establishing a culture of law and

*order, where crimes are punished, and people
are deterred from committing them.*

*Local officials use the grants for a range of
things, from hiring more police officers to
buying new police cars, computers, and even
bulletproof vests. Some communities use the
money to fund public safety programs to help,
for example, at-risk youth or to combat drug
use.*

Countries are defined by borders which are
guarded to protect the sovereignty of that nation.
Immigration law refers to the national statutes,
regulations, and legal precedents governing
immigration into and deportation from a country.
Cities and states have no authority to supersede
federal law.

"Let's take a look at NAFTA. Trump said that NAFTA was a bad deal and he was going to get rid of it in the first 100 days. Now, that's also off the table. He's made a lot of promises that he can't keep. He has distorted information. I do not think he should not be president of the United States. And I think our allies and people in other countries are looking at America and saying, "This can't be. How did this happen?" **(Maxine Waters)**

The President does not require support from congress or any other body to end NAFTA. The decision would be his alone. In the 6 years following the adoption of NAFTA, 800,000 jobs left the U.S. for Mexico.

The implementation of NAFTA removed tariffs, a surcharge that governments put on products from other countries. This has an effect of lowering the costs of goods and creating an even playing fields for all countries. It is believed that the lower cost products have stimulated new jobs in the U.S., but the overall analysis is neither a significant rise or loss of jobs in the U.S.

The world is not engaged in this debate because it does not affect anyone outside the 3 countries covered by the agreement. The Trump administration's goal is to renegotiate the treaty not cancel it. It has however used the threat to leave the treaty to influence negotiations.

President Trump isn't alone in his criticism of NAFTA. He and Bernie Sanders shared many of the same beliefs about global trade deals which they argued hurt working Americans. Sanders called NAFTA and TPP "disastrous" trade deals during his campaign and criticized Hillary Clinton for her waffling on her trade stance.

The goal of NAFTA was to bolster the economy of Mexico, Canada and the U.S. Canada has benefited to a small extent, Mexico has benefited to a large extent and the U.S. did not experience much change.

NAFTA is neither good nor bad. Maxine Waters seems to be embracing NAFTA to obstruct the Presidents renegotiating efforts.

Maxine Waters voted against NAFTA and its predecessor CAFTA.

***"My take is this. The Republicans control the Senate. They have the majority of the House, and they have the White House. They can do whatever they want to do, really."** (**Maxine Waters**)*

Maxine Waters assumes that everyone votes along party lines. If this were the case, then yes, she would be correct, using her logic. Any vote, requiring a simple majority, would be controlled by the Republicans. But people are individuals and may not agree with specific issues and vote their conscience over party line.

More serious issues require a super-majority vote (2/3) to pass. One party cannot pass these issues alone. These include any change to the Constitution, overriding a veto, suspending the rules, ending a filibuster, calling for a constitutional convention, ratifying an amendment, ratifying a treaty, postponing a treaty, expelling a member of congress, impeaching a President, and removing a President.

Ms. Waters is claiming Republicans can do what they like because they are the majority, yet she continues to call for the President to be impeached, although he has not done anything impeachable and her knowledge that a 2/3 vote in her favor would not happen.

*"I think Hillary and Bill are really liberals at heart. I think that, in addition to being liberals, they are very practical. They have made some decisions about what it takes to win." (***Maxine Waters**)*

It is a pretty safe bet that Hillary and Bill Clinton are liberals. Waters was referring to the election and Sanders being so far to the left that Clinton seemed less liberal than she is.

The key for Clinton was not to be great for liberals but simply acceptable to them so that they wouldn't move to someone like, Joe Biden who, could theoretically have made a serious challenge to the former Secretary of State conditions were right.

Clinton's leftward lurch was cast as a transparent attempt to court liberals (far left) and to snuff out Sanders's chances.

The most interesting part of Waters' quote is, "… in addition to being liberals, they are very practical". The inference is that liberals are not normally practical.

"That's what mayors do. They lobby Congress to provide resources for their city." **(Maxine Waters)**

Primarily, cities get their funds through taxation and licensing, though there are other sources of income that cities rely on. Taxation might involve sales taxes, property taxes, corporate and business taxes, and the like. Licensing can cover any controllable resource, from fishing and hunting licenses to liquor and food licenses for restaurants and bars.

Many larger cities also rely on federal or state funding for large construction projects, school systems, hospitals, and other public goods, or depend on money gathered from citations and fines for various public infractions.

If any mayor is lobbying the U.S. congress directly it is either because grant money that had been promised is being revoked or the city has mismanaged the money they have. It is not common practice for mayors to lobby congress.

Bibliography

America Rising PAC. Maxine Waters: Congressional Corruption All-Star. 2016

Bader, Hans. "Clinton Pressure to Promote Affordable Housing Led to Mortgage Meltdown." Competitive Enterprise Institute, 16 Sept. 2008

Charters, Justen. "These 5 Acts of Kindness Reveal There's More to Donald Trump Than Just His Celebrity Persona." IJR - Independent Journal Review, Independent Journal Review, 2 Nov. 2015

Coca, Onan. "Democrat-Maxine-Waters-Caught-Another-Corruption-Scandal." Sons of Liberty Media, 16 Apr. 2017

Glum, Julia. "Six Reasons Why Trump Fired Comey." Newsweek, 22 May 2017

Gray, Madison. "The L.A. Riots: 15 Years After Rodney King." Time, Time Inc., 27 Apr. 2007

Lucas, Ryan. "Los Angeles Sues Justice Department, Joining Other 'Sanctuary Cities'." NPR, NPR, 22 Aug. 2017

Malkin, Michelle. "Maxine Waters as Resistance
     Leader? What a Joke." National Review, 26
     Apr. 2017

Mayo Clinic Staff. "Temper Tantrums in Toddlers:
     How to Keep the Peace." Mayo Clinic,
     Mayo Foundation for Medical Education
     and Research, 28 July 2015

McLaughlin, Dan. "Comey Wasn't Investigating
     Trump - But Look Who Said He Was."
     National Review, 8 June 2017

Mehta, Jonaki, and Sonari Glinton. "Before
     Hollywood, The Oil Industry Made LA."
     NPR, NPR, 5 Apr. 2016

North, John. "LA Riots Anniversary: Firefighters
     Recall Dangers." Eyewitness News, ABC,
     27 Apr. 2012

P., A. "Breaking News: Maxine Waters caught
     red-handed in corruption scandal." Env
     news, env news, 26 apr. 2017

Phillip, Joshua. "After Maxine Waters Says She
     Will 'Take Out' Trump, GOP Opponent
     Calls for Her Arrest."
     Www.theepochtimes.com, 23 Oct. 2017

Schmidt, Susan. "Waters Helped Bank Whose
     Stock She Once Owned." The Wall Street

Journal, Dow Jones & Company, 12 Mar.
2009

Vespa, Matt. "Raging Waters: I Don't Support
Trump Firing Comey, But I Would Have
Supported Hillary Doing It." Townhall,
Townhall.com, 11 May 2017

Wolff, Alan. "What China's Currency Devaluation
Means for the World's Trade Deals."
Fortune, 19 Aug. 2015

www.ingramcontent.com/pod-product-compliance
Lightning Source LLC
Chambersburg PA
CBHW050929260726
48660CB00001B/465